FIRE VOICES

Poetry by Sheldon H. Clark

DEDICATION

My brother
Jared S. A. Clark

In Memoriam
Our parents

Lucy S. Clark, M.D. and Sheldon D. Clark

who gave us life, helped shape our character, inspired us to seek Truth, justice and peace, and encouraged us to be of useful service to others.

ENDORSEMENTS

Fire Voices illuminates the interconnectedness of the human experience. The content of Clark's poetry is easily relatable. Each poem allows readers a wide reach into their ears, heart, soul, and toes. I am particularly struck by Clark's visceral imagery and cunning use of sound and cadence to engage the senses. I am taken on an imaginative journey that is satisfying whether it be: thrilling, uncomfortable, funny, joyous, macabre, deeply sad, uplifting, questioning. *Fire Voices* is a wonderful collection of poems. I offer a caution to the discerning reader; you will be moved by the emotional power these poems tender.

Amber C. McPhail, B.A. Earlham College, 1998
Chatham, New York

Occasional poetic thoughts may occur to any of us when something truly strikes a chord in us, but few of us have the focus and skill to craft that thought into a coherent word song of a poem. Sheldon Clark has that disciplined focus and skill to make his insights accessible to us and we are the better for taking time to reflect on his poems. May his poems reach a wide audience willing to savor these little gems.

Susan I. Swanton, AB Harvard, 1963
MLS Columbia University, 1965
Retired Library Director, Rochester, New York, 1965–2003

Sheldon Clark's latest work operates magnificently on two levels – one the intimate reality of love and loss, the other the wisdom of spiritual maturity and acceptance. Clark asks the reader to join him in bringing these threads together, to experience the loss that comes from endings yet revere the magnificence of life and connection. Ultimately, with his characteristic deliberate language and astute allusions, Clark suggests there is hope to be found in the divine, in nature, in God, and in quiet contemplation.

Sarah Woodside, Ph.D. Boston University, 2016
Associate Professor, Northeastern University

Copyright © 2022, by Sheldon H. Clark
All rights reserved

Published by Rock's Mills Press, Oakville, Ontario, Canada
www.rocksmillspress.com
For information, please contact us at customer.service@rocksmillspress.com.

All imagery is sourced from Public Domain or by Amber C. McPhail

PREFACE

The poems in **Fire Voices** reflect spiritual seeking and echoes of life's challenges and tragedies. **Fire Voices** reveal emotional and spiritual pain, seeking the Divine, observing nature, and expressing hope. The poems are written in free verse. They are unconventional expressions of human encounter, observations of the natural world, and testaments to the process of spiritual maturation. **Fire Voices** challenges readers to explore their ever-expanding interior and exterior horizons. The following hymn has been particularly formative to my development as a poet and spiritual person.

Sheldon H. Clark

Dear Lord and Father of Mankind,
Forgive our foolish ways!
Re-clothe us in our rightful mind,
In purer Lives thy service find,
In deeper reverence praise.

Drop thy still dews of quietness,
Till all our strivings cease;
Take from our souls the strain and stress,
And let our ordered lives confess
The beauty of thy peace.

Breathe through the heats of our desire
Thy coolness and thy balm;
Let sense be dumb, let flesh retire;
Speak through the earthquake, wind, and fire,
O still small voice of calm!

John Greenleaf Whittier (1807-1892)

ACKNOWLEDGEMENTS

VERBA DOCENT EXEMPLA TRAHUNT
(Words Instruct, Illustrations Lead)

Key to the publication of **Fire Voices** are seekers and sojourners, skeptics and the convinced. I am grateful to the following for their technical support, editorial suggestions, and sustaining encouragement: Mary Brewer, Christina Brookes, Jared Clark, Melissa Grimaldi, Sofia Grimaldi, Angela Hill, Marcy Hull, Phil Huynh, Bruce and Betty Ann Jansson, Glenna Janzen, The Rev. John F. Lockyer, Barbara Brown MacDonald, Ella Mallett, Roberta McGregor, Amber McPhail, the late Neil Paul, The Rev. Dr. F. Gardiner Perry, Dick and Betty Preston, David and Christine Richardson, Jane Robertson, Beverly Shepard, Susan Swanton, Charlotte Washington, Carol Leigh Wehking, Don, Harriet and Sarah Woodside. In addition, I extend great appreciation to David Stover, Publisher, Rock's Mills Press.

I am especially grateful to, Amber C. McPhail, who envisioned artistic possibilities within the poetry with charm, sensitivity, and immense creativity.

Sheldon H. Clark, D. Min.
2022

Previous Publications

Poetry and Prayer Sketches, by Sheldon H. Clark with George S. Keltika, 2013
Voices Extended, by Neil Paul and Sheldon H. Clark, 2016
Still Voices, by Sheldon H. Clark, 2020, 2021
After the Fire A Still Small Voice, by Sheldon H. Clark with Catherine Farquhar, 2022

CONTENTS

Dedication
Endorsements
Acknowledgements
Preface
Contents

WELCOME

Opening Prayer
Fire Voices
Heart Speaks to Heart
Bread
Contemplative Worship

OUT AND ABOUT

Teacher Profile
Thoughts on Non-Violence
Aghast
Mary's Song
The Village Play
Sensitivity

FAREWELL

Meeting at the Shore
Spark of Quartz
Haiku
Mystical Sacrament
Closing Prayer

WELCOME

OPENING PRAYER

*Let the words of my mouth,
And the meditation of my heart, be acceptable in thy sight,
O Lord, my strength, and my redeemer.*

Psalm 19:14

God of Light and Love,
We are grateful for Your Presence.
We are grateful for leading us
on paths of adventure, reflection and learning.
We are grateful for reminding us
that You are ever-present, especially
when we encounter disappointments, disasters, and death.

Bless us to become
Your head, heart and hands
In this world.

Amen.

FIRE VOICES

They brought skills
Shared kindling
Solo spirits

They brought silence
Sentinel awareness
Serious purpose

They brought uplift
Surprise
Suspension

They brought light
Security
Surety

They brought others
Singular
Sympathetic

They found space
Stone
Stump

They settled
Silence
Solace

They listened
Synergy
Stir

The Lord was not in the wind: and after the wind an earthquake; but the Lord was not in the earthquake; and after the earthquake a fire; but the Lord was not in the fire: and after the fire a still small voice.

*Vavasor, a feudal tenant.
The term is used here, symbolically, as the tenancy of inner pride.

Confessions, by Augustine (354-430 C. E.),
referring to having a "heart to heart" with God.

HEART SPEAKS TO HEART

Discover Heart

Seek serene vistas.
Nurture becoming.
Explore afar.
Budding time is anytime,
Anywhere,
In its timely rituals of
Learning, testing, affirming, maturing.
Discover vivacity's hope and promise.

Discover Evil

Follow instinctive survival proclivities.
Experience reverses
Via life's doubts and fears.
Convert the vavasor of pride. *
Confession,
Existence by itself, is found wanting.

Discover Life is Lived for the Other

Seminal horizons call to
Find the way to the Way.
Wealth, power, position do not reveal Truth.
Expect abundance, new life.
Encounter integrity, harmony, radiant beauty.
Struggle. Emerge, then soar.
Discover *cor ad cor loquitur.* **

Give us this day our daily bread.

Matthew 6:11

BREAD

Breads, like people, broadly speaking, defy absolute definition.
Samples are swirled mementoes of throat-sized clusters, which
titillate palates from home to across the seas and sustain life.

Bread bits crunch, sizzle, and sparkle as the staff of life.
Breads precede us from breakfast to the cocktail hour
enhanced with sour cream, marinated onions, and pickled herring.

Breads, unleavened, yeasty, moldy, penicillin conveyors
are honored by health-conscious dutiful types,
who commune during lunchtime and enjoy hasty noshes.

Breads hold hot sauerkraut and warmed pastrami or corned beef together,
between mustard slices, but come apart if held too long,
with fingers washed three times afterwards and again later.

Breads are the warm harbingers of simmered sausage gravy,
Of butter and jam, of cheese slices, and help to wake up
the mornings with hot drinks, and then may complement afternoon tea.

Breads are aromatic essential dough, firm, soft mulches of ornamental,
oriental, and occidental offerings, cooked black, brown, beige, and white
on electric stoves or gas, over dung, or wood, to give it that extra bit of savory.

Breads of wheat, rice, millet, cornmeal, and other flours
are like the folks, who eat them.
They are ever-fascinating, tantalizing, mercurial, rich, spoiled, soft, hard,
between assignments, ubiquitous, and are enhancements to our lives.

CONTEMPLATIVE WORSHIP

Be still and know that I am God.
Busy thoughts swirl.
Do this. Do that. What's next? Set priorities. Delegate.
Children's needs. Spouse's needs.
Chores. Meals. Dishes. Cleaning. Dusting.
Sweep the porch. Weed the garden. Mow the lawn.
Bank. Gas up. Grocery. Pharmacy.
Compose a mental laundry list. Anticipate the morrow.
What happened to down time, social-time?

Rest in the Lord, and wait patiently for him.
Quiet the mind. Choose a center, then focus.
Choose animals: sleeping puppies, grazing horses, pollenating bees.
Choose vegetables: snow peas, ears of corn, carrots, turnips.
Choose minerals: gold, silver, lead, alabaster, marble.
Choose visions and dreams: peace, serenity, justice.
Choose memories: family, siblings, education, trips, vacations.
Choose prayers: familiar ones, extemporaneous ones.
Choose emptiness: nada, nothing, naught, zilch.

They that wait upon the Lord shall renew their strength.
Seek comfort in body, mind, and spirit.
Seek that which is good, true, and beautiful.
Seek silence, the sacred, the sacramental, reflect.
Seek the holy. Not me, but the Other. Pray for others.
Seek the nonce. This time is time out from the hurly-burly.
Seek stillness in heavenly calm to be present in this moment.
Seek out a deeply personal image: a ring, an embrace, a dream.
Find the aura of inner peace.

Let not your heart be troubled.
Bless those who are ill, fearful, worried, anxious, angry.
Bless those who need intervention.
Bless those who are in transition.
Bless those who are controlling.
Bless those who are in doubt.
Bless those who seek.
Bless those who are sick, mourn, hungry, poor.
Encounter your contemplative key that ignites inner serenity.

Psalm 46:10. Psalm 37:7. Isaiah 40:31. John 14:1.

OUT AND ABOUT

TEACHER PROFILE

So, teach us to count our days that we may gain a wise heart.
Psalm 90:12

Great teachers teach people, and love their chosen vocation.
Great teachers admit to mistakes as opportunities for learning.
Great teachers champion differences as opportunities for expanding horizons.
Great teachers employ self-evaluation. *"Know thyself,"* Socrates.

Great Teachers Assayed

Friendly
Kind
Patient Empathetic
Problem Solvers Respectful
Warm Well-groomed
Organized Articulate Sensitive
Smiles
Encourage Caring
Listens Sense of Humor
Disciplined Courteous
Likes People Nurture
Scholarly
Genuine
Professional Team Player
Positive Cooperative
Enthusiastic Compassionate
Interested Energetic
Involved
Questing
Sense of Values Appreciative
Personable Knowledgeable
Emotionally Stable Inquisitive
Perceptive Motivate

Great teachers liberate the "Teacher Within."
Great teachers are travel companions in search of Truth.
Great teachers inspire future generations to do and be their best.

AGHAST

Aghast at the Indian Residential Schools 'buried child' grounds
condescended to be identified as unidentified.
Graves occasionally marked with a Christian Cross
As though these premature deaths held meaning,
hardly expresses the outrage.

"Jesus wept."
He is still weeping two thousand years after
His own crucifixion at the horrific sacrilege, contempt,
disregard, antithesis of his New Commandment,
"Love one another as I have loved you."

Aghast at mollifying explanations proffered.
No negation, disavowal, counterpoint
mitigation, palliation, assuagement
is justifiable to explain deprivation, starvation,
disease, physical, mental, emotional, spiritual abuse.

Shame, disgrace, infamy, mortification, indignity,
intentional denial of genocide, and apology are absent.
Any professed high ideals, or sacred professions,
or holy representations, or transcendent experiences,
disappear and dissolve into the mists of forgetfulness.

Abusive power leads and feeds excessive brutality.
Dehumanization, inquisitional torture, denial, occur
when truth requires admission, confession, disclosure,
recovery, reclamation, participation, involvement,
decency, acknowledgement, reconciliation.

Antipathy has cause to grieve, feel despair, know hatred.
Acceptance is not a ceremonial handshake.
Mercy is not an element in the initial equation of resolution.
Forgiveness is not a first thought for action.
Love is not an immediately forthcoming quality.

Knowledge and wisdom hope to lead to seasoned hearts.
Power in Compassion is two-directional.
Angry fearful inner fire is quenched by generosity of spirit
Needs cross is the horizon's mirage of coexistent possibilities.
Time present, remembrance of times past, shall embrace time future.

A voice is heard, lamentation and bitter weeping.
Rachael is weeping for her children;
she refuses to be comforted for her children,
because they are no more.   Jeremiah 31:15

MARY'S SONG

Conception and Birth
My son, conceived in holy love, was born to serve.
He was Zacharias' and Elisabeth's nephew, John's cousin.
He, too, was a miracle child as announced by the Archangel Gabriel.
Nazareth, our home, was subject to Roman occupation, taxation, and power.
Jesus' birth in Bethlehem, was into an uncertain and violent world.
I worried, would he even live, and grow up, even after our flight into Egypt?

Babyhood
Our son gradually found his place, as a child will.
He nursed, laughed, gurgled, burped, slept, and laughed.
He crawled and walked like a seafarer.
He imitated what he heard and saw and discovered in his own voice.
He formed complete sentences and asked questions.
He scratched his knees, fell down and stood up into caring hands.
He found his inner voice and spoke words of Truth.

Early Life
Our son grew up, was adventuresome, self-confident, and known to be wise.
He helped build affectionate, respectful, and caring relationships.
He found joy in simple natural things and among varieties of people.
He contemplated our world and worlds beyond our experience.
Where did he go?

Young Adult
Our son found hospitality in neighboring villages.
He followed streams into the hills from whence he emerged serene.
He seemed able to live a fulsome life unscathed by worldly pleasures.
He visited the Jordan Valley and the shores of the Sea of Galilee.
He was so like others, yet, he was so different.

Adulthood
Joseph and I were constantly amazed.
Our son saw the Light for us to see, too.
There was no adolescent rebellion, simply a profound maturation.
Our son helped us beyond expectation and found companionship everywhere.
Our son gave love as he had been given love and more.
Our son prayed so that others would never fear from want again.
Our son was grounded in the undefinable Spirit of God's Presence.

Death
I saw his death, too. Horrible.
Ironically, I felt a Light in the darkness of his ending.

Resurrection
I saw the beginning of his Eternal Life as in a dream
I felt his power of love reach immeasurably beyond time and space.
I knew in my heart that His death was only the beginning.
God's Presence is as it was in the beginning is now and ever shall be,
world without end.

THE VILLAGE PLAY

I sat still
reading
on the loud night.

Drums
From beneath the idols' tree
from the village center
beat
announcing the Ramayana
to be enacted
by dark-skinned,
thin,
Long-haired
Gypsy men
and their
full-voiced hungry daughters,
where with ingenue beauty,
they would sing
in the entre actes
collecting paisas
in colorful handkerchiefs.

Between the sun-worn
white-washed temple
and the idols' roost
orange muslin was
draped over
a rickety
bamboo frame.

Gaudy costumes
decorated
old women
and ancient mystic-men
as they enacted the ancient
Sanskrit drama of Rama/Sita vs. Ravana.

Back in my chair I could only marvel
at what I had just witnessed, an
abduction saga from a bygone past.

The next morning
Under that same tree
Boys were pitching
Moonstones.
Only ox dung
Told that a pageant wagon
had stopped.

Maybe in that
faded memory, the reality of
oxen needing to be shod brought focus.
The strong short blacksmith's portable bench
was covered with half-moon ox shoes,
trimming tools, nails, and hammer.
Three teams and their drivers waited.
Industry as usual happened in the early morning
under the cool shade of
the idols' tree.

SENSITIVITY

Creation positioned
Not quite, almost, yet
Nourishment, gentle amniotic bath
Umbilicus working in rhythmic accord
Time contracted over time in time
As though for the first time, this time
Calm turbulent waves sought, fought to arrive
Relief, recovery, again-and-again, then intense
Wonder.

                                  Placental vessel calls, superfluous
                Breath, breathe, strengthen, start, sleep, stand, search
                      Wobble, instinct, rest, arrive, a willing life
                          Encouraged, pacified, respired, evolved
                  Hesitant, like a budded green flora apple opening
                      Hard, hidden, tenderly, reaching, opening
                              Lit, sighted, striving, wet, warm, dry
                                    Evolutionary metamorphosis

Steady, protect, watch, care, warn, accept
Sensitivity needs, intuited in silence
Aware, alert caress, nuzzle, bond
Know help, shape, mold image on image
Distinct individualistic and symbiotic
Nourish, relief, recover
Eternal design recurrent
Soon mortal radiance cavorts, enough
Well Being.

Consensual partnership matures
Point by counter-point play, decade by decade
Enhancing deep spontaneous hearts
Beating as one indivisible
Recognition, unconditional validation
Us, we, bond with subliminal devotion
Naturally, our entwined vines meld as one
Evident by love, joy, peace, patience, kindness,
Goodness, faithfulness, gentleness, and self-control ... finally final rest.

Against such things there is no law.
Galatians 5:22-23

FAREWELL

MEETING AT THE SHORE

Meeting at the shore,
Serrated sand favors water lapping,
Enhanced by an aspirant lyre.

He strummed his harp.
They embraced an enchanted future.
Eternal dance begun; cruelly fanged.

She, consigned beyond the River Styx.
He, petitioned; issued a caution.
Doubt. Breach. Cessation.

Lyre silent. Devastated.
No more the enchanting promise.
No more the ethereal sway.

Illusion, reality, entwined
The hesitant moment,
Knew finality.

Warm sand shifted
Below the ebb and flow.
Rippling traces appeared, vanished.

Intimate incandescence winked from ocean's
Meniscus to deep down darkness,
Left no doubt.

No assignations anymore.
Eonian music vanished. Panoramas gone.
No meeting at the shore.

Time present cast asunder.
Awake, anguish to
The irrevocable liberation.

Stroll. Stop. Turn.
Mirages envisioned vanish.
Prevailing westerlies wave to a soaring
Fregata Magnificens.

SPARK OF QUARTZ

Deep down there where the sun does not reach
A spark of quartz, a glimmer of hope, a star twinkle
And yet, the shadow of uncertainty, a trick of the eye
Hesitant, inevitable, sure, definitive
Conjured the myth again and again.

Where is gentleness in the discourse?
It trips speculation, the banter, the give-and-take, the exchange
Would you? Could you? Please? The plea sounded
From the depths, rippled to the surface
Shimmered in the fickle hunter's moon.

They went swimming in an open irrigation well of expectation
Careful block and mortared walls held in and held out
Artesian bottom, step-to-steps-to-steps, breathe above water
Excitement, curiosity, known and unknown beckoned
Venus and Adonis, Orpheus and Eurydice, Jack and Jill.

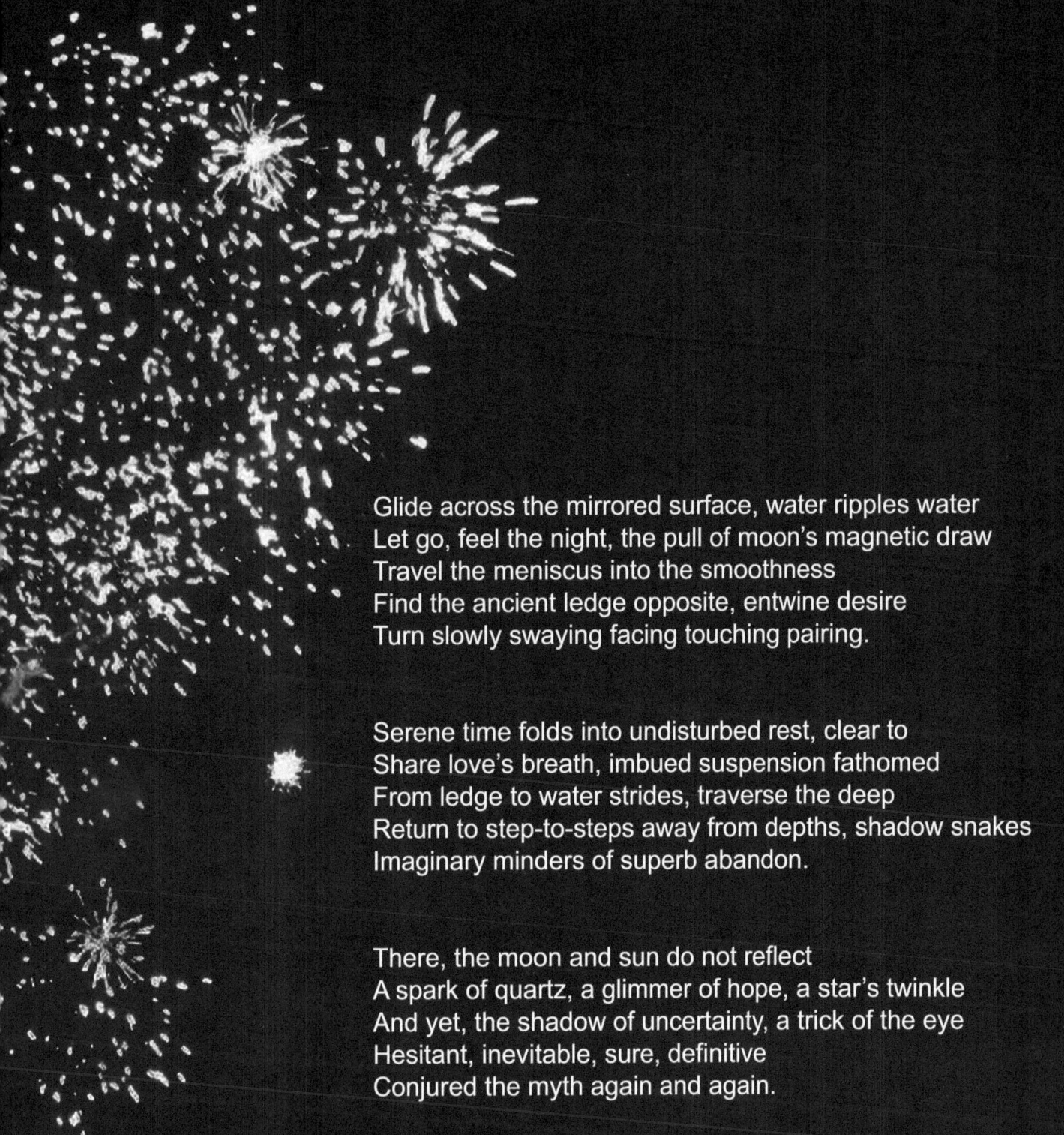

Glide across the mirrored surface, water ripples water
Let go, feel the night, the pull of moon's magnetic draw
Travel the meniscus into the smoothness
Find the ancient ledge opposite, entwine desire
Turn slowly swaying facing touching pairing.

Serene time folds into undisturbed rest, clear to
Share love's breath, imbued suspension fathomed
From ledge to water strides, traverse the deep
Return to step-to-steps away from depths, shadow snakes
Imaginary minders of superb abandon.

There, the moon and sun do not reflect
A spark of quartz, a glimmer of hope, a star's twinkle
And yet, the shadow of uncertainty, a trick of the eye
Hesitant, inevitable, sure, definitive
Conjured the myth again and again.

HAIKU

Make a joyful noise unto the Lord, all ye lands.
Psalm 100:1

I
Fog waves mystery
Warm baking bread fills sky's glow
Waiting sun's tableau

II
Mortality true
Bubble's lift, hereafter, truth
Reveal moon tides

III
Wind rustling blossoms
Steps slip past quietly
Leaf fluttering

IV
Light play dances
Bird flight soars grass waits at peace
Shallows invite trout

V
Since my love is lost
Other friendships bloom, succulents
Share fresh legends

MYSTICAL SACRAMENT

They Aspired Presence
Capacity
Intelligence

They invited friends
Acquaintances
Strangers

They congregated gently
Seeking
Yearning

They brought concomitance
Intention
Reserve

They sought Light
Tranquility
Calmness

They envisioned encounter
Potential
Serenity

They became Joined
Devout
Reverent

They found
Enchantment
Wonder

When he was at table with them, he took bread, blessed and broke it, and gave it to them. Then their eyes were opened, and they recognized him; and he vanished from their sight. They said to each other, "Were not our hearts burning with us while he was talking to us on the road, while he was opening the scriptures to us?" Luke 24:30

CLOSING PRAYER

Dear God,
Astronauts view this magnificent globe
as sea and land, cloud cover, and clear blue.
They verify what the rest of us
can only imagine, and yet, imagine we will.
Our world is a magnificent creation
of balance, proportion, cosmic beauty.
Humankind is rediscovering
its affinity with Mother Earth.
We pray that all may enjoy
Creation's munificent bounty.
We pray for the intriguing possibilities that
physical, emotional, psychological,
and spiritual health
can bring to our planet and everyone on it.
We thank you, God, for life.
Amen.

www.ingramcontent.com/pod-product-compliance
Lightning Source LLC
Chambersburg PA
CBHW040020130526
44590CB00036B/37